BLACK and WHITE
Animals

Zebras

by Mari Schuh

CAPSTONE PRESS
a capstone imprint

Little Pebble is published by Capstone Press,
1710 Roe Crest Drive, North Mankato, Minnesota 56003
www.mycapstone.com

Library of Congress Cataloging-in-Publication Data
Library of Congress Cataloging-in-Publication Data is available on the Library of Congress website.

ISBN 978-1-5157-3374-4 (hardcover)
ISBN 978-1-5156-3393-5 (paperback)
ISBN 978-1-5157-3397-3 (eBook PDF)

Summary: Learn about zebras!

Editorial Credits
Gena Chester, editor; Kayla Rossow, designer; Morgan Walters, media researcher;
Kathy McColley, production specialist

Photo Credits
Newscom: TUNS/picture alliance / Arco Images G, 21; Shutterstock: AppStock, 17, BMCL, 7, Curly Pat, design element cover, Ehrman Photographic, 1, GTS Productions, 11, GUDKOV ANDREY, 19, JHVEPhoto, 13, Markovka, design element throughout, nutsiam, 9, paula french, 15, PHOTOCREO Michal Bednarek, cover, Richardlightscapes, backcover, Villiers Steyn, 5

Printed and Bound in China.
009958S17

Table of Contents

Lots of Stripes 4

Life in a Group. 10

Glossary 22
Read More 23
Internet Sites 23
Critical Thinking Using
   the Common Core. . . .24
Index. 24

Lots of Stripes

An animal eats grass.

See all the stripes?

It's a zebra!

Its mane has stripes.

Its tail has them too.

mane

A stripe can be wide.

It can be thin.

Life in a Group

Zebras live in Africa.

They live in a group.

This is called a herd.

Look!

A mom gives birth to a foal.

It walks in an hour.

Zebras are fast.

Zoom!

See them go!

Chomp!

Zebras eat grass.

This is called grazing.

Gulp!

Zebras drink water every day.

They fill up!

Zebras groom.

They pull out loose hair.

All done!

Glossary

Africa—one of Earth's seven main land masses

foal—a zebra that is less than one year old

graze—to eat grass or other plants on the ground

groom—to clean and make an animal look neat

herd—a large group of animals that live together

mane—long, thick hair that grows on the head and neck of some animals

Read More

Kuskowski, Alex. *Zebras.* Zoo Animals. Minneapolis, Minn.: Abdo Publishing, 2015.

Moldovo, Eustacia. *Baby Zebras at the Zoo.* All About Baby Zoo Animals. New York: Enslow Publishing, 2016.

Peterson, Megan Cooley. *Zebras are Awesome!* Awesome African Animals. North Mankato, Minn.: Capstone Press, 2015.

Internet Sites

FactHound offers a safe, fun way to find internet sites related to this book. All of the sites on FactHound have been researched by our staff.

Here's all you do:
Visit *www.facthound.com*
Type in this code: 9781515733744

Super-cool stuff! Check out projects, games and lots more at
www.capstonekids.com

Critical Thinking Using the Common Core

1. What activities do zebras do in groups? (Key Ideas and Details)

2. How do zebras take care of themselves and one another? (Key Ideas and Details)

3. Why do you think zebras need to run so fast? (Integration of Knowledge and Ideas)

Index

drinking, 18

eating, 4, 16

foals, 12

grooming, 20

manes, 6

herds, 10

stripes, 4, 6, 8

tails, 6